NATALIE COPELAND

WHEEL

Written, illustrated, and published
by Natalie Copeland

For more information about ordering,
reproductions, and author engagements,
contact the author via her website:
www.nataliecopeland.net

Edited by Evan J. Peterson
Art Direction by Kaitlin Dempsey

ISBN: 978-0-578-64132-4

To All
who stay up watching meteor showers
who wake early to summit by sunrise
who hug and talk to trees
who look to the stars for guidance
who treat moments as adventures
who occasionally follow joy too far
and love too hard
but who always get back up.

ACKNOWLEDGEMENTS

Many of the pieces in this work are inspired by real trails, all of which are on Indigenous land. Before proceeding, I must pay my respects to elders both past and present who have stewarded these lands, and who continue to honor and bring light to them.

I must pay my particular respects to the **Duwamish** people, from whose unceded lands I currently write, and to the **Snoqualmie** people, whose watchful mountains have gently raised me, whose powerful waters have moved right through my living room, whose trees have patiently listened, and whose mists always call me home, home, home.

If you love these lands, there are many ways to be a good steward. All aspiring adventurers and romantics would do well to familiarize themselves with the principle of "Leave No Trace," but if you would like to go a step further, consider donating to or volunteering with your local trail organization.

Finally, this work is equal parts adventure memoir, graphic novel, poetry anthology, autobiographical journal, and scientific grimoire. While many pieces are based on real people and events, their fragments have been culled from the last decade, and as such, do not represent one person or event. I would like to acknowledge the forces that have led me to this work, if only for providing a mirror with which to better see myself.

Our mythic heroine's story is one that should be as familiar as any fairy tale in the modern age: it is the cyclic, spiral journey to the center of oneself. And as with any myth or fairy tale, you may choose to read this story literally or metaphorically. Either way you would not be mistaken. Sometimes a hike is the change, but more often it is just the catalyst. It's your story.

CONTENTS

I

II

III

Larch March

IV

V

I

Woodland Cathedral
Spring, Dirty Harry's Balcony Trail

Let's breathe.

Let's place our feet in the mud
and count the birds' songs
not with numbers
but with souls.

Let's let the branches speak to us,
the moon flood our skin,
the sun flood the land,
the flood chisel the river,
and the bed grow to include us.

Let's watch life
so precious
pushing on differently,
just a little changed —
Soon we succumb
to the same.

Let's laugh in assent
    that we come from the sun,
    sister the moon,
        and become the mud,
    the bud,
    and the branch
that the circadian chatter of birds
    will serenade
        as we breathe.

undone

I have learned to love the quiet moments
when it's just me
dragging my toes across the fitted sheet,
petting one long, silky leg with the other,
fingernails tracing familiar paths
down familiar roads,
longing to quench their thirst for life
and the things they can't touch.
With skin taut and tingly,
and core soft and warm like butter,
I am squirming with secrets unspilt,
deeds undone,
and havoc unwrought,
waiting for a magic word
or touch
to come undone.

starstirred

I wonder if it's possible
to love the stars
as fiercely as I do
without loving love just as fiercely.

There is a stirring so steep
and so intimately connected to my whole
when I am under their spell —
not unlike the song of my **heart in heat.**

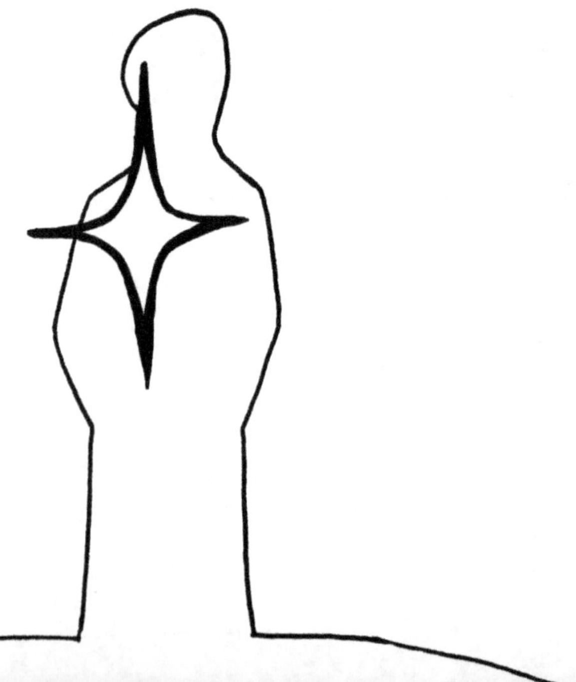

drunk

As Baudelaire said:
"Be always drunk,
on wine, poetry, virtue,"
or what-have-you.
And after sobering
from aurelian dawns
and whiskey-drenched stars,
I find solace in the tipsiness
of irreverent magic eyes
from the bottom of a margarita
or a paint-stained enigma
from behind a glass of red.
Slowly, carefully, languidly,
Quietly,
Flirting with possibilities
of being drunk once more.

The Graceful Lament

The thing is,
you can't ignore that graceful lament—
the teal heaving of your chest—
the wash of questions in your head
that exquisitely hold pinpricks
of the future.

There's a brand of groan you know well
that belongs to feeling unresolved.
That noise you make
when you're a painting without a face—
when you're two lines of a song
that's lost to the wind—
when you're a cup of water
dribbling through careless hands—
that noise is the growl of restless dreaming.

There is a struggle to unpin yourself
from the avalanche of time
that has pooled thickly around your legs.
You try to kick, but it moves like molasses—
slower than a hard thwack
to a non-newtonian fluid
and pointless as collecting antique doorknobs.

There is an urge
to catch destiny by the tail
as if you're somehow prepared
right now —
as if there's nothing left to learn.
How fortunate you are
that perceived linear realities
can curve the hubris of your fantasies.

And yet
there's that gnawing need —
a craving that demands surrender —
that all too graceful lament
of being forced to take
the smallest of steps
on the greatest of adventures.

butterflies

Oh that we were not creatures
Sometimes so in tune with our world.
My stomach is telling me
That **something** must **happen** today.

tectonics

I can pinpoint the day,
the place,
the hour,
and the clothes we wore.

You stood too close
as you murmured a joke,
and the scent you wore
filled my head
as I laughed and laughed.

I marvel that this subtle quake
could set everything in motion,
and yet,

I've been **adrift** ever since.

ships

I have a hard time with differentiation
between "getting coffee"
and "Let's demolish 3 bottles of wine!"
between "getting inspired"
and "Let's spend holidays seeing the
        country in a van!"
between "getting butterflies"
and "Let's kiss on the face right now!"

Surely,
there must be spectrums I can bisect
splitting
Platonic from **Romantic**
Sensory from **Sensual**
and **Casual** from **Committed**
but they are not immediately apparent
to me.

Nevertheless,
all ships must be properly cared for,
so I will patch the holes,
man the sails,
and try not to rock the boats
too terribly hard.

I Am Loud

I am **loud**
demanding attention,
I know when I am being **charming**
because I try
I put on my impressing face
and do my impressing hair
and speak my impressing **words.**
I **tell** you my embarrassing drinking stories
and everything else about me
that you probably don't need to know.

I am not the sweet girl
who will leave you with a smile
or a touch
or a glance
or a single **word.**
There is nothing of this fashion of romance
about me.

I am someone who will **point** out your flaws
and take you out to see the stars
and **remind** you of your humanity
and what a wonderful thing it is.

I am someone who will **press** you
about **music**, sciences, histories, and **words**
and point out the constellations, beaming
as I teach you their **names.**

I am someone who will **voice** puns
with no regard for quality or obscurity
and **recant** how I once left school
to join a troupe of clown strippers.

I am someone who will stand on a table
and instigate highway **sing-alongs**
and transform into a **wolf**, or tigress
and run up mountains.

I am someone who takes too many shots
and **coaxes** you to bed on a Russian liver
and knows all the right places to bite and tease
just for the exceptionally coherent **pillow-talk.**

I am not a silk scarf on the wind.
I am not a thing hard to capture.
You will not spend a perilous journey
through a wild, perfumed jungle
searching for my slender garments
hung beside a pool
as I **wail** to the breeze.
Rather,
I am a bird flying overhead
making too much **noise**
with strange and vibrant plumes
distracting from the trail ahead.

I am many things
but I am not quiet.

Of this I am sure.

trick candle

You sparkle
atop sheets of frosting and promise
and I am drawn,
so drawn
to your flame.

But I am old enough to know
that candles are pretty, temporary things,
impossible to keep burning,
meant for ritual and decoration alone.
I snuff out this silly idea
and set you aside,
ready to take the cake.

But then
there you are again,
a trick candle
catching my napkin on fire.
Inconvenient —
but I'll bite.

Being with you

means I don't have to imagine
what it would be like
and I can just be.

Being with you
means I don't have to worry about
what you really think,
when to time my words,
or if you'd kiss me.

I know that
you will tell me what you can,
my words can tumble without stopper,
and we won't touch.

My wild imagination
must be tamed
or it will plumb the deepest depths
and climb to treacherous precipices.
Being with you
pacifies this beast.

Being with you
is always better, brighter, and steadier
than I imagine.

I just want...

I just want
to throw our backpacks in the backseat
and take a careless adventure,
Wild —
Jovial —
Unbridled —

I just want
to take you out from this fencing
into new surroundings once more, abandoning
Labels —
Structure —
Facades —

I just want
to admire your work
that you have shaped with
your Hands —
your Will —
your Individual Cut —

I just want
to take you out
to the open road to see
    what you would Shout —
      How Reckless you would be —
        what Abandon you could
          inspire in me.

I just want to feel the Earth move with you.

shift

It is a strange moment —
a change in the wind, perhaps? —
a shift ever so slight
when your eyes drift skyward
and you brightly propose,
"It's nearly the season
for us to go stargazing!"
      — that this time
I do not dally through the valleys
of misplaced nerves and doubt,
before laughing, sighing, and shrugging,
"Yes! We should! Well... Goodnight!"
      — that instead
I send my eyes aloft
to meet those flecks of dreams and dew,
before laughing, sighing, and shrugging,
"Well... How about tonight?"

In May

In May
the forest
erupts
in aromas.
"Did you miss me?"
it teases.

The mountain
peaks
denuded
of white shawls
flirt
with the sun.

My body
subsists
efficiently
on fruit,
nuts,
and clear, cool melt
in May.

Gravity

I struggle to hold myself up
(to a standard, to an ideal,
of self-care, self-respect,
and protection of heart)
but this is a slide
that I have no power over.

This force that pulls me —
(yes, this very idea has gravity)
— this force is unrelenting,
gnawing, sneaky, persistent,
not intentional or malicious,
simply inevitable.

It is a slow erosion
taking a mountain out to sea
when I look,
and a great landslide
swiftly collapsing
when I turn my back.

Where once
I hung precariously,
I was at least secured
in a temporary equilibrium.

Now
just one cord snaps
and I am swinging,
falling,
a safety net not yet woven.

Gorge-ous River of Light
Summer, Columbia River Gorge

moments

There are moments that wake you up —
that knock you squarely
from what once passed as reality
into a new frame of being.

These are the moments
when the Milky Way
snaps into perfect clarity —
when a breeze off a creek
whispers the cyclical secrets of its past —
when perfect music or perfect silence
replaces the voices in your ears —
when your hand is held with care
and you're electrically grounded —
when you're suddenly in existential peace
with all of your fears.

These are momentary lapses in the definite —
brief flashes of eternal significance
in the obvious meaninglessness of life —
moments that transcend the inevitability of death —
a reason for existing in a reasonless existence.

Trail

We don't have to walk far
under the cover of canopy
to find exposure.
Once outside the city,
outside the usual framework,
outside the boundaries of polite necessity,
we can truly breathe.
On the trail
I bathe in dust
and my hands converse with trees
when asking for support.
Nursing logs remind us
where we stand
in an ancient cycle,
and we can confess anything.
Stripped down to our bare humanity.
It is the intimacy
I used to chase in pillowtalk
but without the dance.
The trail is always a soul's journey
whether solo or shared.

I close my eyes

to make it as dark as I can,
to shut out the light from the hall,
   the street lamp,
      my alarm,
to make it as dark as the sky
that we lay beneath.
I re-populate the darkness
with the pinpricks we know so well.
Would you give me permission
to do more than imagine,
to accompany you out to the open dark
of the plains and the mountain tops,
if only to spend the hours it takes to get there
voices alight,
learning your favorite things,
and then hours under the stars
in awestruck silence?
Excited breathing. Buzzing. Elation.
A late and innocent night
on the edge of dawn.
I open my eyes
to the headache of the hall light,
   the street lamps,
      my blinking alarm.

Veritaserum

If I'm being honest,
I press my lips to the glass
to follow you down.
I am a message in an opened bottle,
but I keep pace
with your sips,
hoping our loose lips
might, together, launch ships.

If I'm being honest,
I sip the nectar of intoxication
to make excuses.
I am sure of my sober thoughts,
but I know
under night's tender spell
is where we might tell
all truth before morning's knell.

If I'm being honest,
I'm already one ahead
to calm my racing heart.
I have rehearsed this conversation alone,
hoping to finally break
past the short ending
and through the faltering and shaking
to say the things we are longing.

If we're being honest,
we're getting toasted
just to loiter.
We keep turning the hourglass over,
buying more time
with water in bars,
playlists in parked cars,
and chilly walks under the stars.

birds

The birds residing in my heart
did beat their wings with such force —
there was nothing but the beating —
so many beats all out of sync —
Throbbing. Thumping. Racing.
Finally, I opened my mouth
and one by one they each did fly out,
and soar,
and my heart grew lighter.
After many hours,
one by one they returned to roost,
folded their wings, and tired,
tucked back into my heart.
A mass of gently moving, feathered bodies,
whirring with a soft, electric hum.

Exhausted

My makeshift mattress beckons,
and I have saved half a bottle
of companionship and comfort
for tomorrow's adventure.

There are frustrations and exhaustions
sewn throughout my brain
but now is the time
to put them to bed.

Tonight we spend long hours together
spilling childhoods and chilled liquor,
keeping the night bright,
and wrapping ourselves in laughter.

Tomorrow we venture forth,
face down our differences,
and search for some new way
to fight back the dark...

After we sleep.

rare kind

He is a rare kind
with rare kindness
so he'd never
in a moment
of electrostatic tension
close the gap
between our lips.

And truthfully,
it has been so long
and I have learned so much
about consent
and ruined friendships
that I don't remember how.

enchanted

"I could live here,
In the mountains,"
I say,
anytime I go anywhere
with mountains.

The words are involuntary.
No spells have been cast,
yet I am enchanted
for better or worse.

"I could go there,
anywhere,"
I say,
any time you say
you want to go.

angular

Watch me
and I am a **wheel** —
always finding a way
to **spin** anything into gold.
But given just the right **moment**,
and just the right rush of **speed**,
you will see me as I truly am:
a **gyroscope**,
my **angular momentum**
keeping me upright.
And you—
you are always the right **rush of speed**,
and it is always the right **moment**.

Like treading water

Like treading water —
like waking from dreams
to find the day hazy and surreal —
like the inability to stem
the begging hunger
that threatens to rend
polite tasks asunder —
is waiting to return
to the mountains
and real life
with you.

secrets

Are there secrets at the bottom
of this bottle here to savor?
And are they more commensurate
to its volume, or its flavor?
Could ascetic tongues here loosen
and become more libertine?
And could cold feet here defrost,
performing dances unforeseen?
Oh, I think that we should try it —
drink me underneath the table,
for I have no use for secrets,
but I'll trade mine if I'm able.

hazy

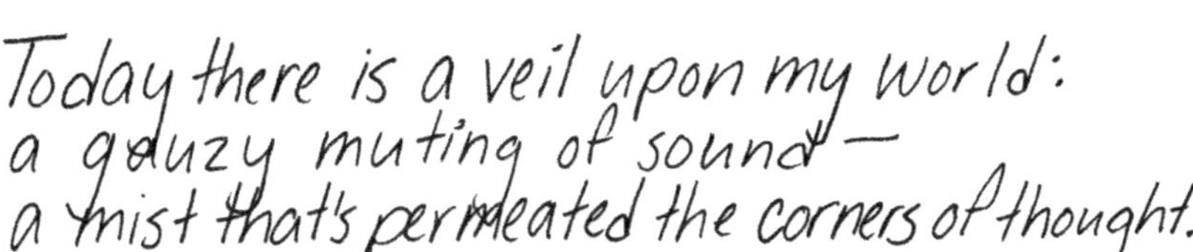

Today there is a veil upon my world:
a gauzy muting of sound —
a mist that's permeated the corners of thought.

I know there is a crisp clarity outside:
a pounding passion in the sunlit world —
a million hues to roll in and embrace.

My tingly thought centers all recede,
rejecting stimuli like adventurous taste buds
recovering from exciting, scalding tea burns.

I just have to remember and accept:
sometimes there are going to be days like this.
Lazy, hazy.

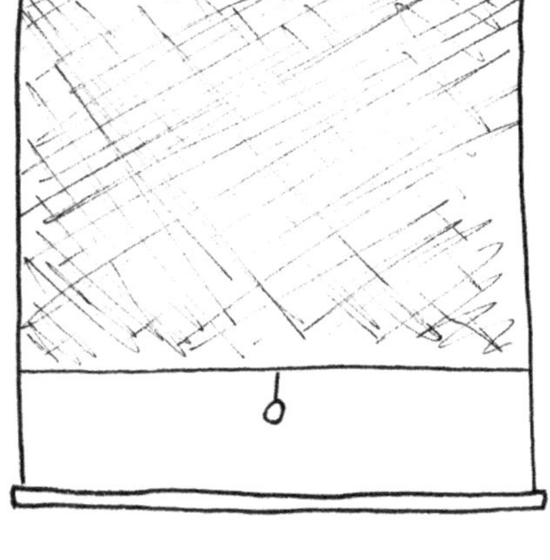

filthy

In the summer,
hands in soil,
bodies covered in dirt,
running barefoot,
camping in grass,
rolling in mud,
smoke in our hair,
dust in our socks,
tasting the Earth,
juice dripping down chins,
flowers in hands,
rolling down hills,
resting in roots.
In the fall,
rain in our hair,
rain in our clothes,
rain on our skin,
rain carries filthy rivulets
to the drain.

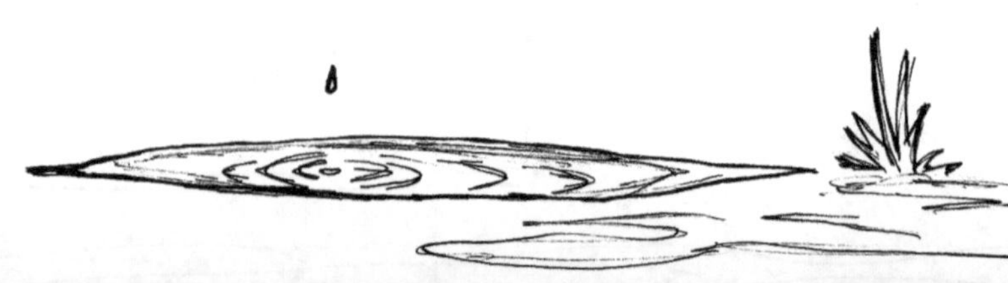

Oh, Summer

Oh, Summer,
would that you would make me your bride,
for I'll come back to you endlessly,
body and soul
brimming to full
with the deepest parts of me
both at peace and at play,
consistently
sun-kissed,
wind-blown,
soaked in halcyon brightness
to the bone,
this divine passion
never fully served
by memory alone.
Oh, Summer —
my truest love,
would that with you I could stay,
for I hold you in my heart year-long,
and pine all the while you're away.

meteors

We burn like meteors:
hot, fast, and bright
screaming through the atmosphere,
hearts afire, souls alight,
each trip
One small skip for heart,
One giant leap for meteorite.

But there are two inevitabilities:
time
and with it, gravity.

We break apart,
losing light,
we extinguish,
losing sight,
but after it's over —
after it's gone —
I'm still
euphoric.
High.

Replays shooting through my mind —
I begin to suffocate on oxygen.

I desperately search
for a laugh or a sound,
hoping a new voyage
will soon be found,
grasping at wind
all the way down,
just a stone in thin air
plummeting to the ground.

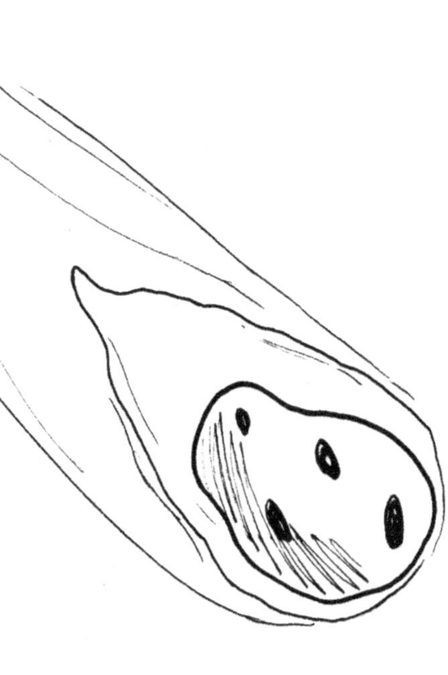

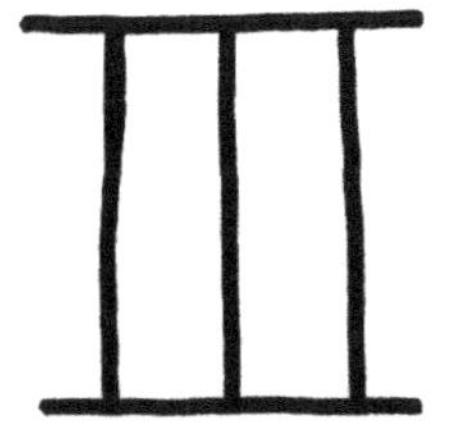

Larch March

Fall, Cutthroat Pass

precious

The sun sets more quickly each eve
by mere perceived fractions,
but each time I am more aware
of the preciousness of breath.

Cycles

The Sea of Tranquility descends tonight
into waning, gibbous shadow.
As I bear witness to the sight
I can't help but wonder —
how many moons
have I waited and watched,
and which cycle signals
the end of this working?
My rituals greet phases
full after new,
celebrating faces
both blood-red and blue,
eclipsing even the sun
from full view.
It seems by now
the spell must be sown.
And perhaps it has been —
for while I was watching
I certainly have grown.

oh.

Finding twigs in my hair
from where I impulsively
rolled in the grass.

Ha.

Should have known
that days of summer
were too good not to pass.

Travelers

I beam when leaves stick
to the bottom of my heavy leather boots
as I tromp from one place to the next,
delighted when they're still there
after every sticky step.

I dream
that leaves must have a yearning—
after fastened so long
and working so hard—
to see the world.
The wind whispers,
"I am here to bear you anew,"
and the leaves surrender,
fluttering to the ground,
then back to the air,
then back to the ground,
tumbling merrily
in their twilight hours.

When leaves stick
to the bottom of my heavy leather boots,
I like to think that I've aided
in fulfilling a dream,
like scattering ashes.
I've shown them a new world
if only a hundred feet away.

fever

Ferry ride.
Puget Sound.
Sweltering delirium.
I want to unwrap my skin.
This fervor consumes me.
On the prow of the deck
I gaze into the terminator
dividing open air and rain.
A stoked frenzy.
I need to flush this flush
in numbing chill.
A temporary calm in me
as the temperature drops,
but this fever has less chance of breaking
than the clouds.

scorched

My cheeks are scorched
by the fire in my blood
and words begin
to well within.
But my courage is scorched
by another fire
that's damned the well,
and I can't begin.

breakable

It is a moment
so delicate
that eventually
a single heavy breath
and slice of light
will crack...
But for now
it is a hushed dawn
so breakable.

prayer

Way up on the mountain,
pumped up with endorphins,
at such elevation,
breathing anew,
I collapse with elation,
by my wondrous companion
and with determination
devour sandwich (and view)
and every last sorrow
drains
    out
        of
           me.

I heave a long, tender,
whispered prayer:

"Bliss and only Bliss.
This and only This."

electrified

The fresh memories of
the impossibility of your words,
the incandescence of your eyes,
and the intoxication of your lips,
come in flashes,
running down my prickling neck,
through my tingling core,
and to my trembling toes.
They are small bolts of lightning
striking the same place,
over and over and over —
infinitely unlikely —
shocking, shaking, and grounding,
all at once.

expensive

Honesty comes at a price —
but so did the countless rounds
of glasses, boxes, bottles, and cans
that we purchased
while searching for a substitute.
We may be in one hell of a mess now,
but at least we'll never
have to drink that much again
just to spill our hearts.

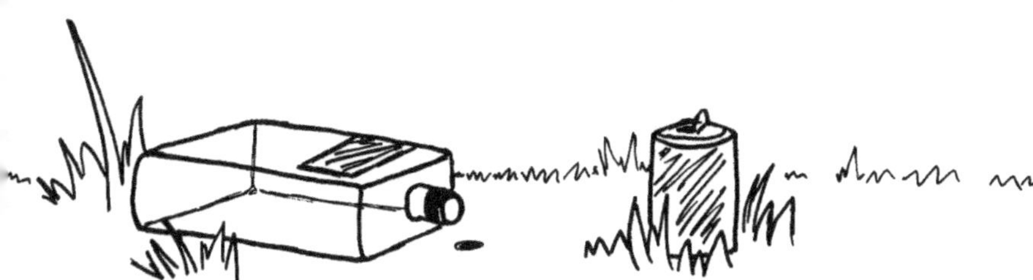

jolt

I still need the occasional jolt —
a pinch —
a reality check —
to wake me
from the dreaming world
of long-held hopes
suddenly manifested.
I try writing it all down
and replaying all that I remember —
revelations, hands, scents, astral bodies —
and I just fall deeper
into the unreal!
So for now
(absent that jolt)
I'll make do
with the occasional buzz
from my pocket.

Scorpio Season

It is Scorpio season
in every possible sense,
for there is no safe, solid,
middle ground to stand upon
that hasn't been wet-soaked
with its flood and blood
that transforms the gentle earth
to obfuscating mud.

But then, perhaps, it is actually clay
taking shape under a vision in silver,
for the full moon in Taurus also glides
across these charged, erotic, Scorpio skies.

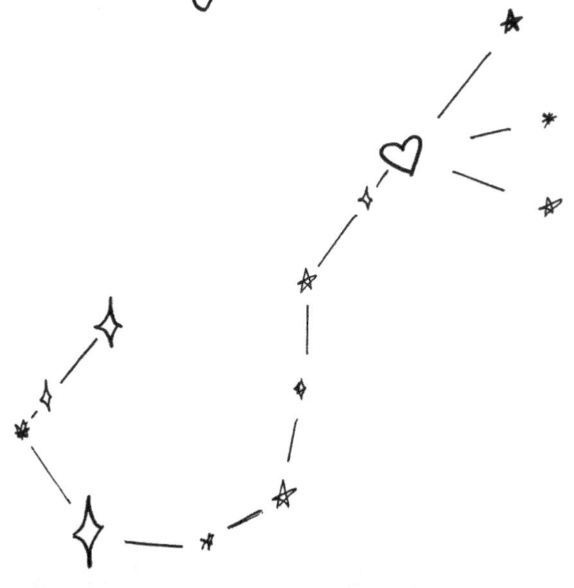

timber

I need air —
    I need earth —
    I need water —
but each breath is too shallow,
and this bra is too tight.
My chest twangs —
my slipshod lumberjack
sinks his axe into me
and I find myself split —
taken to the ground —
without warning —
harvested for my
Precious Heartwood.

breakups

Perhaps I take breakups,
and half-breakups,
and "I think we should just stay friends,"
and "I'm moving across the country,"
and "Let's just hit pause,"
and "I'm busy that night,"
and the vacuum of communication
so horrifically,
and yet so horrifically well,
because on some level —
lover, friend, or stranger —
I am always romancing
then losing
the idea of everyone.

eclipse

It was purple and silver
shadows and smoke
It was bright flashing beads
and perfect syzygy
It was collective breath held
released in wild cheering
It was subversion of night and day
It was waking up
It was religion
- an affirmation
of things long-well-known.

And it was fast
Faster than imagined
Over fast as it began
My eyes blotted but briefly
But vision shattered evermore

Every moment unbelievable
        but true —
        in the Total Eclipse of You

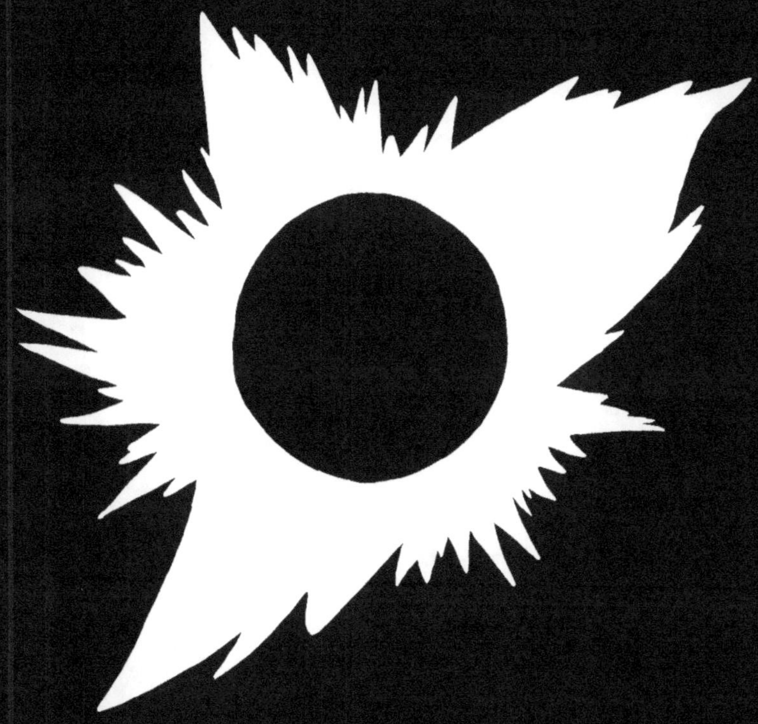

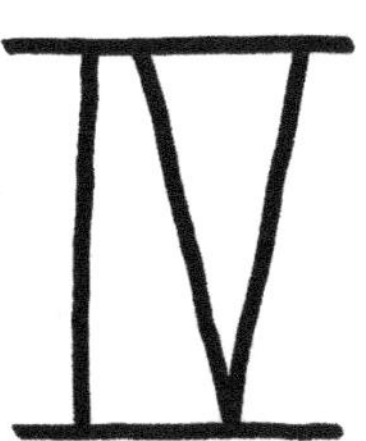

Mist Opportunities
Winter, Commonwealth Basin

74

sleepless

I have woken up too early
for a sun that shall not rise,
and my dreams have flown with moonlight,
leaving cold and clouded skies.

Maybe next breath,
next hour,
next sun,
or next moon
I'll be warm?

It is far too dark for hope — and still —
I must, somehow, hope that I will.

Survivors

Freezing fog,
trees protest,
they can't shiver,
it's a test.
Wait for spring,
hold all breath,
patient trees,
denying death.

Stagnant air,
hanging white,
building daggers
in the night.
Grim to breathe,
grim to touch,
patient are trees
that suffer such.

Winter cracks
and winter cleaves.
No bitter words
are heard from leaves.
Watch the trees
for they will show
the path of patience,
and way to grow.

Venus in Aries

It must be maddening,
if not terrifying,
to be loved by me.
Attempts to temper me are useless,
for I can only love with flames
burning hot, bright, and white
like dazzling stars,
until smouldering embers
ignite everything I hold dear,
leaving brittle, black scars in my wake.
Even now,
as the dreams I clutched too closely
crackle and crumble,
my cheeks burn,
flushed with embarassment and anguish,
and the grieving pouring down them
is so hot,
it could boil and steam.
My stomach churns with heat,
and I am a dragon heaving forth hell.
I am too impetuous, impatient, imprudent —
a relentless, tempestuous firestorm.
I am too many words too quickly —
a meteor shower of **poetry** and **regret**.

stuck

When pins and pressure plates
crawl into my spent shoulders
I clutch madly
to crush the offending sinews.

When I've grazed the side of my tongue
with an accidental death threat
I revisit the spot and repeatedly incise
until I'm sucking crimson and tears.

When the she-squito shoots me up via
serrated needle and turns me feast-like
my fingernails compulsively scavenge
out the adenosine deaminase.

I sniff the arid bottles of perfumes I love
that are no longer manufactured.
I re-trace my lost friendships
through the riverside paths we fashioned.
I chop onions and slurp hot sauce
until I'm dry.

Maybe that's why I'm stuck on you.

climbing

It's as if we're climbing
over mountains,
except by some cruel trick
we trek along the fault line
rather than across,
and as we crest each painful saddle
there is no choice
but to slide back down the other side,
blistered,
   limping,
      starved,
        and carrying too much weight,
hoping the next peak
will be the last.

Except
it's nothing like climbing mountains,
for at least in the mountains
I can breathe.

pretending

The days that are the most full
are the days spent pretending
we weren't waiting.
Our organs churn like machines
producing twice their expected amount
of free-flowing adrenaline,
which we give a task to circle,
rather than the drain of lonely,
gut-wrenching "what-if-tomorrows."

There's the waking struggle
of swinging your feet from your bed
and testing your floor,
and hearing a scream bubbling
forth from the lethe,
tickling at the daybreak,
and knowing that you must
wrestle, mash, and toast it
into a tasty breakfast morsel
lest it overwhelm the dawn with
restless shadows.

We drag the lengthy hours
through the mud,
fatiguing their thread,
living mercilessly,
until they no longer resemble time,
but immeasurable, intangible everythings.
There can be no counting
of patchwork days —
only the art of making them count.
It's a productive little distraction,
so we can pretend that we're not waiting.

toxin

The poisoning isn't always painful,
like a rattlesnake, or arsenic.

Sometimes

it is a whisper
soft and sweet
like a lullaby singing "carbon monoxide"—
too much fun too quickly
as you slip into a black overdose—
a poppy-soaked dreamland.

Sometimes

it is a fragment of truth
that was real once
but exists now only as memory—
the thing you want to hear
picked out of the words spoken—
a misguided make-believe.

Sometimes

it is a song we both love,
the night we heard it,
and the memory I built around it —
a cloying clawing
corrupting with a buzz and haze —
a saccharine toxin to the imagination.

reminder

The photo you took
and then gave to me
still hangs framed
above the altar,
next to the calendar.

Should I have taken it down
when your words slipped away?

Perhaps.

But it hangs as a reminder
to hope
for Lovely, Wonderful,
Improbable things.

first snow

Silent, unexpected ripples
as the first flakes softly alight on the lake.
A crisp inhale with eyes closed
followed by joyous vaporization of cloud.
When vision flutters back into focus,
a spectacle ever-more lovely than the last.
The muffled crunching around the trail,
near-muted chattering of chipmunks,
windy flurries whistling then growing placid,
the softened screech of a hawk
subdued now to an awed whisper,
mounting and falling like a Debussy.
Clearer and more humbly triumphant
than cathedral bells.

This suite—this bright panorama—
shows me to the brink of an elation within
and brushes my crystalline spirit.
It sings and I overflow—
light pours drop by rapturous drop
from each eye.

Wait Training

I keep saying
"This would be so much
more bearable if..."
But maybe
it isn't supposed to be
more bearable.
Maybe I'll train
and find new ways
of bearing it.
Maybe I'll feel
that much lighter and stronger
when the load is lifted.

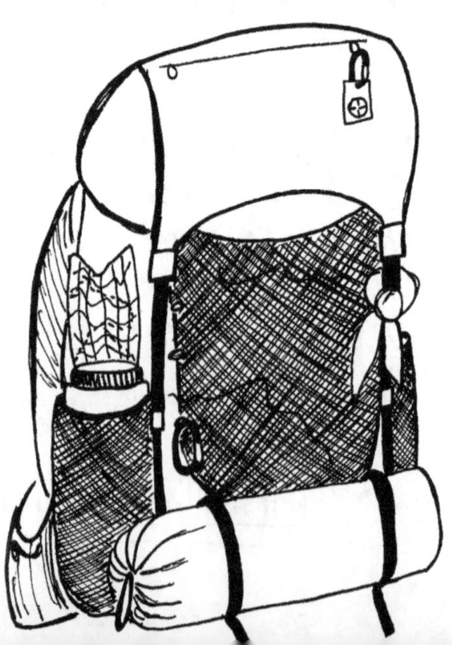

Still

A reminder —

It is still winter,
we are still in the thick of it —
chains and snowshoes
are still requisite —
Imbolc and Candlemas
are still to pass —
groundhogs hibernate,
tarns still as glass —
the tumbling finch song
has yet to be sung,
and even the false spring
has not yet sprung.

So lie still a while longer,
let the chill freeze you through —
warmer days will return
in their own time,
and so will you.

Fly for $178 roundtrip!

All of my targeted ads remember
that we wanted to go to Iceland
in winter
to see the Aurora Borealis,
and they bombard me relentlessly
as if marketing in memories.
This instance is not unique.
It seems
no matter how many buttons I push
in attempts to subdue
these bright incursions,
I can't mute you completely.

deeper

I have let my inbox fill,
let my hair grow long,
and moved the cup
that once collected my life
(that constantly ran over,
spilling drops to the ground)
to the side temporarily
so a deeper vessel can be found.

But I'm not worried —
I'll be around.

Winterkill

I am no gardener, but I do know this:
perennials and orchards need the kiss
of an early frost, a freezing deep,
to hold them whole through winter's keep.

A bloom in false spring, winter's hollow,
before the heavy snows that follow
will have the cell walls bursting, cracking,
freezing, thawing, expanding, contracting.

So too, must dreams lay dormant still,
or else become the Winterkill.
Much as I wish them to bloom, bloom now,
they must lay under the mulch and bough.

I tell myself,
"Learn what you can from the season,
Patience, myopia, acceptance sans reason —
you are stuck in the wheel, right here and now,
hearing naught in the dark, muffled underground."

Yet I am no seedling! I am no tree!
(Though my flesh warms and cools just as easily)
So why should I wait? Why be pinned by the cold?
Do I have a choice in the story that's told?

Could I be a cold crocodile, nose above ice,
Or hibernate warm with the marmots and mice?
Why not come in from the outside to thaw,
And savor small tidbits of hope in my maw?

Could I choose to fly south, or to stay evergreen?
Must I really wait for the melt to be seen?
I wonder, though I'm sure what seed I am from,
Is it **winter** that dictates what I will become?

Riverside Baptism

First sun-warmed sand,
first boots-and-socks-off beach,
first ankle-deep stand in rushing water,
first SPF rubbed on my face,
first crocus pops up in the yard.
(Delicately)

Nearby, a young father begins
to teach his toddling young
how to fish.
(Patiently)

Last high-country snowshoe,
last low-country wood stove fire,
last hot bourbon toddy,
last dreamy days in Pisces,
last longing for lost love melts away.
(Finally)

Early over the mountain,
the nearly-but-not-yet Worm Moon
spies the confluence below.

Here at the place where things change,
the wild world fills me
and I devote myself once more.

For one who is in love with the chase
and the glory of all things yet-to-be-done,
the true rapture of Nature is in knowing
She is too Big, Wild, and Free to be won.
(Like me)

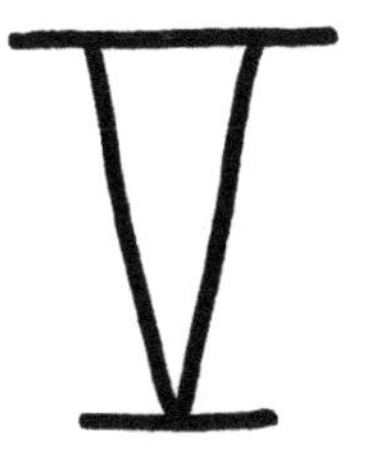

Eruption of Color
Spring, Mount St. Helens

Pink galoshes

I hear it before I see it —
a steady everywhere-roar.
A sleepy tumble
to slide the slats of blinds
confirms:
turbulent and torrential
puddles seem to leap
ever-so-slightly skyward
with each wet wallop.
It is the determined,
slantwise
rain of change,
blustering with purpose,
washing winter woes.
I dress —
    Pink Galoshes —
    Pink Slicker—
    Pink Smile—
to greet this
Gray April Shower.

The road ahead
is full of possibilities,
but not for the faint of heart.

Luckily,
I am not faint of heart.

Burn Area

Take quiet, reverent steps
through these charred steeple spires,
and listen for the roaring echo
of an event so fierce —
so nightmarishly tragic —
that we must soothe this loss
with such assurances as
"Everything has its own time," and
"This ecosystem needs fire."

But nothing needs lightning,
systems are products of conditions,
and life doesn't thrive on tragedy —
it exists in spite of it.
Just as we are not born in space
and yet we hurtle through it,
so too does bright fireweed spring
between these spindly, blackened corpses.

Tide

All those moons ago
I plucked a stone from shore
and whispered my intention
with each waxing and waning.
I took it back to the Sound today,
intending to sing a final goodbye
before casting it far into the waves.
It sparkled in the spring sun
then slipped from my fingers
into the sludgy low-tide pool
of barnacles and q"ideqs.
I simply walked away
and watched the gulls drop oysters,
fighting over what belongs to whom.

The waves will carry the stone to sea
the same way the green has returned
like the green in me.
A gentle and abrupt easing —
a slip out with the tide.

gift

Give yourself the gift
of a day alone —
a day of your own making —
of singing madly,
scribbling passionately,
eating well,
listening deeply to your own desires,
and sitting with your own folly.

Give yourself this,
and you will never feel loneliness
as an insurmountable ache
again.

He Was A Kaleidoscope

I chose to look closer into him than most do.

My discernment found worlds in him
that most would not.

I clung tightly to pages of mystery
bound by him-ness,

grasping at tendrils of smoke and mirrors

looking between our hands for a
hidden universe.

And then
quite suddenly
I saw him:

Just skin and words and memories
I'd simply been looking through
to find reflections of myself.

My ribcage:
full,
then hollow —
snatches of memory,
then fear —
press,
snag,
then release —
like breathing —
heavy,
ponderous
breathing.

Instructions for Wind

Call me to the mountains once more,
oh sweet, murmuring gusts,
and remind me who I am.

Sweep up my laughing toes to the tops
of these proud outcrops,
then give my breath to the dome
when after looking out,
I see not my city,
but my home.

Bring forth the rich perfumes
of startling everything-ness
from the valleys,
and after I have drunk the proud skirt
of these verdurous hills,
let your sweet touch guide me up,
and pin my head to thy scoping bed.

Then hush, let me be as I espy
my gentle, distant, giant lovers,
dependably rising from the East,
with supernal gossiping
for my cognizance alone.

Let me imbibe their wisdom
until all my queries and qualms
slip from my eyes,
dissolving into secrets
and thanks beyond measure.

One last request,
my swift-flowing friend:
wipe these wet lessons from my face
and carry their essence to the edge—
to Karman,
and meet the angel
who waits without air
to carry my cosmic missives there.

I have made the night mine,

no longer asking,
"May I accompany you?"
Instead, inquiring,
"Would you like to accompany me?"

I have made the forests mine,
no longer requesting,
"May I show you this place?"
Instead fielding,
"Will you show me this place?"

I have made the mountains mine,
no longer begging,
"When shall we go?"
Instead,
filling my calendar,
filling my backpack,
filling my heart
with what is mine,
and going.

The Hike

--My feet are big
and growing ever bigger.
Large, wide,
and filling every shoe.
They stick out from me
making flats look ridiculous.
They are life rafts,
falling to the side like pillows
when encountering resistance. --

My feet are long
and growing ever stronger.
Supportive, storied,
and deserving special care.
When pointed, they are elegant—
skeletal and muscular, even when in heels.
They are canoes,
chiseled and carved with love,
gliding forward with intention.

Almagest

I have had enough of lovers
wishing to be the sun in my sky,
standing far too close for comfort
and blocking half my dome at a time.

To shine with such effulgence
should be an honor all my own.
Who else is my constant companion?
Who else keeps my dreams aglow?

Instead, let all that is loved by me
be a dazzling array of constellations.
Each brilliant Sirius and Betelgeuse
whirling, returning through my seasons.

And if I should find such a Star again,
let them be not my Sol, but Polaris—
gleaming steadfast in their own region,
never dipping 'neath horizon's terrace.

Their simply existing
a northward guide,
keeping me truthfully
aligned.

wayfinding

Above all
I thank the stars
for the gift of wayfinding.

The gift of terrifying awe
as Orion's belt peers through the trees,
bringing South.

The gift of sure confidence
as I point the Dippers out to others,
bringing North.

The gift of guesswork
as we discover behind which peak
the sun will rise, bringing East.

The gift of inevitable hush
that descends along with her,
bringing West.

The gift of heavy elements
composing all,
and my body,
and these eyes
that were also made for
reading maps,
reading animal sigils,
and reading signs.

Above all
I thank the stars
for teaching me
to find my Self
in the world.

Wheel

Do not expect a linear path
nor a strictly circular one
though you meander one foot to the next
in cyclical, somewhat predictable rhythms.
Do not expect clouds to behave,
mountains to hold,
or branches to grow.
Do not expect bridges to stand the test
of time that even trees cannot.
Do not expect your golden shot today
to hold your interest your next go
round the wheel.
Do not expect a clear and simple reward.
Rather,
take what you can
whenever you can,
drink it in,
and make it a part of you
for the next go round.

Shepherds of Wonder

I stand on the precipice —
feverish yet clear —
shaking, consumed, saturated —
overlooking the valley of the year ahead
stretched out below.
I must somehow chart a course
using only these distant glances from aloft
which shall be revised again, and again
as I forge my path.
But in this moment,
on this mountain,
all is still.
There are no words.
Only a pure tone
ringing forth from my heart.
It is the quiet breath before.
Before questions.
Before answers.
Only this breath suffused with light.
Only truly being.
This state of awe.
This heaven.

I stand with the Shepherds of Wonder.
The leaders of spirits, hearts, and minds
to places within and without.
Those who can wrangle the
wandering cries into joyous song.
Those who can speak their minds
defending justice in word and deed.
Those wily leaders of sultry passion
who dance the pleasures of flesh.
Those whole-hearted carousers
who invite raucous laughter to exhaustion.
Those who know that truth,
however fragmented,
speaks through passion.
That reality,
however subjective,
is anchored to our place in all this.
Those who know that fear is the arrow
pointing us where we must go.
I stand among them,
gathering the pause,
eyeing and toeing the cliff's edge.

Then suddenly
the swell,
the stirring excitement,
the revving,
the sudden skip in heartbeat
in anticipation of
all future Loves, Losses,
Silences, and Laughter;
the sudden idyllic nostalgia
for all future cycles
yet to pass, into life
and out of time so quickly;
future stories yet to be told
and soon to pass from all memory.
The suspense of the unknowable
in a race against mortality
draws me nearer the edge.

I draw a breath on the outcrop.
Once again,
like the Shepherds of Wonder before me,
I find the spark to journey on
in the calm
before the leap.

CASCADIA

Just like a river, meandering true,
I'm like a river flowing back to you,
From the alpine turquoise to the ocean blue,
Cascadia, flow through me.

Just like a Cabernet, smooth and red,
You're like a wine flowing to my head.
I won't get enough, not until I'm dead,
Cascadia, flow through me.

Just like the city running to and fro,
I'm like the city when I ebb and flow.
Like a train, if I leave, I know back I'll go,
Cascadia, flow through me.

Just like blood, with no end or start,
I'm like the blood flowing back to my heart,
Returning to you, dear, has become an art,
Cascadia, flow through me.

Just like the city train, just like blood,
If you're the soil, I'll be the bud.
Just like the river, just like wine,
If I'm coming home to you, I'll be fine,

Cascadia, flow through me,
Cascadia,
flow through me.

About the Author

Natalie Copeland is a multi-disciplinary artist and space science educator. Born in the Cascade foothills, Copeland holds a BFA in Musical Theatre from Central Washington University, and is known primarily for her work in Seattle fringe theatre. She is passionate about wild spaces, teaching students to stargaze in the planetarium, and adventuring with friends.

Find out more about past, present, and future projects at NatalieCopeland.net.